A Crooked Stile

By the same author:

Poetry
Fishing in the Devonian
X^n

Illustrated Novel
Select Episodes from the Mister Farmhand Series

A Crooked Stile

Carol Jenkins

PUNCHER & WATTMANN

First published in 2019
Published by Puncher and Wattmann
PO Box 279
Waratah NSW 2298

http://www.puncherandwattmann.com
puncherandwattmann@bigpond.com

NATIONAL
LIBRARY
OF AUSTRALIA

ISBN   9781925780499

Cover design by Miranda Douglas

Cover image: Carol Jenkins

Printed by Lightning Source International

This project has been assisted by the Australian Government through the Australia Council, its arts funding and advisory body.

Australian Government

Australia Council
for the Arts

Contents

Flirt

Did we flirt? I can't remember. Fall?
We're falling still.
Patient? Well, waiting doesn't qualify.
People told me so much about you,
and really the only time I saw you truly
was in the pocket mirror of others' eyes
and scribbled notes, then that brief and sinking
rapture of being you, a glancing, giddy undertow.
Take for granted doesn't even start to say.
Still I know I'd be nothing, nothing, without you.

Heart of Snow: Saint Valentine's Day Sculpture

'Volenti non fit endure'

Very fine, the white heart stays put,
its cut-in edge, its frozen veins
untroubled by pulse or impulse,
constant to its plot of ground,
lying in this snow-bound field
without a murmur, until
the season's done, the bare
oaks and tulip wood standing near,
looking on.

Lambertville, New Jersey, USA

Hunterdon County, NJ, in the Imperfect Tense

Empty houses, windows boarded up, wood-sidings weathered grey,
flour mills with peeling paint clustered like hoboes
round a burning drum, postcards foxed by decades, their inky
carte postales fading to paler blue, the reverse a photo
of a woman in lisle stockings, hair marcel-waved
who might be the great-aunt of those diminutive old ladies
dragging shopping trolleys, overcoats cinched tight to wasted waists,
hair fine as floss, faces an architecture of sparrow bones,
pale skin like ancient silk kimonos; roses, blown, just holding on,
each petal faded, soft and stained, ready to disintegrate.

Hunterdon County, New Jersey, USA

Severe Weather

Lightning cracks the sky. I drive
into a void, there is the car, the storm,
the freeway's aquaplane and slipstream,
its static of heavy haulers— their weight a glue
of dubious inertia. Too slow
you're fender fodder, too fast courts
fate. The thing to do is keep on driving.

Now the rain's too loud to hear the radio,
wipers whip-whipple, the outside
is a species of mesmeric convulsion
that improbably continues, cars ford
the foot deep run up to Hawkesbury Bridge,
a turnstile into the river's vortex, faith
here is to believe the road I can't see exists,

its image a convoy of dots and dashes.
The rain beats on and on, the car's a drum
of uncertain pitch, time dilates —
there are impromptu waterfalls but no
time to stare at them at all —
now the pinging of hail,
I try not to fall into its thrall,

a million drops confound the air, fade the world

to grey, into a strange operculum of half-haze

half panic. This is a nexus of craziness,

crazy speed in a swamp of rubber, steel

and motor parts, governed by that tricky

eye, with its blinking lid, that argues

with the brain that claims somewhere

there is a road, and you're on it.

Picasso's Dog

Where the brown paper has been snipped away,
a white dog, ears upright, tail to attention,
eye trained on a dove, holds one foot
off the ground, in a concentrated pause
that has lasted since the brown dog ran off
with the paper dove seven hundred dog years ago.

Barcelona, Picasso Museum

Fire Night: Les Merces

I

The fire eater is addled with metho, stinks of wood alcohol,
sweat, diminishment. He needs money, or air.
He drinks and blows, more, more, till the air is singed
with blue-red plumes and he reels, skin flecked with char.

II

A carrefoc of spark dragons, devils, gothic terrapins blistered from the heat,
smoke swirling, hooded men with pitchforks gushing sparks
of burning metal oxides, antimonies of light craze the night — you dive
under the splinters of broken fire, inhale the sweet stench of salt-petre.

Barcelona

Algodon de Azucar

She wets the stick and waits, watches

the sugar spin into filaments, at first she collects

sweet nothing, then the idea of a dream.

A crimp of sugar cotton floats out like web,

she spins the stick, twists

and winds till the stick is a cocoon —

not liquid or toffee, not syrup or thread or crystal

but a crumpling sweetness, a faintly pink sugar cloud

that dissolves, like time, leaving its memory in the blood.

Port Aventura, Spain

Waiting

I have five minutes to write to you so I'll not
mention, Companero, how I am wanting to hear
you laugh, waiting like a match in a box,
waiting like shoes under the bed, waiting like the spoon
in the drawer ready to dip into the velvet cream of you,
frantic like the white sheets flinching in the wind,
no, I will not say these things about waiting.

Bilbao

Calle de Caballero de Gracia

On a stationary bicycle, the chain engaged
to a dry stone wheel, turned in steady rhythm,
the knife-sharpener of Calle Caballero de Gracia,
without pausing, lifts the blade, blows off
graphite dust, considers its sharpness,
and returns it, curving the blade in even strokes
along the stone, his left hand playing
on slips of air, old legs quickening as stone
and blade rasp out their song.

Madrid

Windscreen

The view is winter, evening —
busy with the traffic's northern peristalsis,
Seaforth and the Spit Bridge's
lights are sliding
slow blurred, down my rain swerved
windscreen, spilling lines of light
over its curb, the bent edge of drops
gregarious in thick bundles of hard water
and water knocking on my car's tin roof
so all the distortions of glass, of angle,
sluice to remake a flattened world
of melting, molten light and rain.

Night gardening, mauve and mutable

One a.m., an alcove opens to show a back lit slipper orchid,
then closes. The orchid had slipped off eleven years before.
The sweet pea seeds that did not make their planting
date with Saint Pat's, bloom midwinter in the sofa divots
while a startling halo of cherry blossom grows
on my head the night I came back from Bundanon.
The ferns do not block the lower steps, that
is their day job — they're only neat by night.
At two am I set to with a spade and plant an acreage
of asphodel in a corner of the garden that day will not reveal.
Night root stocks are pure graft, the peach tree fields cherry pits
inside a plum dark flesh, the scent is apricot, like it too forgets.
The jacaranda blossoms give proof of coloured dreams, like a note
written in early sleep, here, take this as evidence.
The day time trees I planted, the lemon gum in Darlinghurst,
a winter crop of angophoras at Crafers: do I appear in their dreams
trailing clods of dirt, leaving the scent of sweat from a damp
and dirty shirt, and broken vanes of windmill grass?

The Lens

Often, late at night to see
if that small frustrum
of correction, my contact lens,

has been removed or is
still in, when most things
in the room are mostly in focus,

to avoid playing eye-poker
I test for improvement in acuity
the lights at Manly, way across

Middle Harbour, by putting
on my glasses, while wondering
what other shortfalls of perception
this metaphor might stand for.

5th Floor, Hotel Oslo

Late afternoon, six pm, above me an uphill acreage
of terracotta tiles, white walls and high Manueline
windows; a hawk, wings shadow thin, plays
the thermals, feathering the wind. Five
t-shirts; three white, one pink and one-long sleeved,
try their best to fly off their line after him.

Coimbra

You are Now Out of Focus

like the Torre de Clerigo's edges, soft and gothic
from my myopic gazing, a mythic, an up-lit teller
of haunted tales, with its subtly blurred details like the past.
This is the blessing that time gives me, with the arc
of my own hand I can dissolve, to incorrect
the perfect acuities lent to me by glasses, counterfeiting
the ocular girdles of youth's precise vision.
Like those sharp-edged loves of my early days
that I now view through two, or three, sets of lenses.

Oporto

22

Counter Talk

For SN

Unmarry me, so we can meet again
not as in those days with us as fresh

as butter, gold with our light, young people
in long nights of counter talk and pillow fights

tea in bed and more, but as we are now knowing
our years have fled as fast as they were held

so unmarry me, so knowingly, we can wed again.

The Wedding Gloves

We are the second pair of hands, warm companions,
worn to hold another pair. Of course there is the Dress,
oxidised now to a fine faint yellow by the sun, it has no rub,
no marks of wear, save for two small moth holes
on one undersleeve. Worn only at the dressmakers,
then that single time. Maybe it was a little jostled,
one might say given short shrift at day's end,
but we were there for balls and receptions, wedding parties,
civic duties, and later, when less than white, odd times
pressed into a day job, inside her winter coat.
The glove hook knew us well, his adroit trick
of closure. We kept our wrist line, while our fingers
creased at each joint of hers. That bottle of benzene
she had to dab off dirty spots, the odd giddy
whiff on the side, even this proved unequal
to the grime. The little split, right hand middle finger,
hers always the first to push in, the last to leave.
Years now, we have retired to the long box,
just as she has, but we being tanned persist as ourselves,
and of course, we always have each other.

Marrickville Library: The Meek Collection

Valentine

my crush, my love, my aorta, my superior vena cava
my beloved, my dearling, my darkling, my weekday,
my weekend, my small beer, my whatever-ails-you,
my new shoe and its other half, my hot bath
my first, my last, my cup of tea, my breath,
my heart, my honey bunny, my meadow grass,
my in-too-deep, my stolen sleep, my funny,
my favourite dish, my delight, my day and night,
my content, my close-the-door, my flora,
my dizzy height, my laid low, my elephant in the closet,
my chew-the-fat, my pack rat, my one true,
my skip-a-beat, my take-a-seat, my come-here-often
my heart's alarum, my holy ghost, my little devil
my green-eyed one, my fine face, my fellow spoon
my eyes-grow-dim, my him, my hum-along, my song
my mr wrong, my turn, my garden-by-the-sea
my part of me, my ketch, my hawk, my diplomat,
my all-of-that, my time-on-earth, my home & hearth,
my here, my now, my caramelo, my bed fellow,
my light, my laugh, my daft thing, my that thing with wings
my world-go-round, my dog-my-thoughts, my could do worse
my nothing better, my love letter, my hot tomato,
my finders keepers, my first edition, my still-in-print,
my type, my tea and toast, my ever after, my res ipsa loquitur,
my give and take, my gave and took, my pride and broom,
my sing-in-tune, my cloud nine, my parking fine,

my cross that bears me, my ode to autumn, my spring rooster,
my personal pronoun, my prima facie, my turn-the-cheek,
my decade spanner, my monkey wrench, my kitchen's bench,
my seas-gang-dry, my Spanish rain, my can't complain, my cup's saucer,
my hot water, my ritornello, my squireling, my systole, my hyperbole,
my moonbeam's mcswine, my cherry wine.

Running Upstairs, After Seeing Theo off on the Snow Bus

In that state of occupation that might pass
for happiness, I bounce up stairs intent
on all my busy duties, and a line from Dylan
inveigles in its pleasant melody, sweet
and so familiar,
you're going to make me lonesome when
you go, and oh, boy, I stop
mid-stair and cry.

My Daughter's Ear at Sixteen

We are talking about romance as a construct
what it is and how it got to be,
about Emma, and every minute or so I, or she, throws
in an idea into the grinder and gristle it around;
the euphoria of longing, the way literature
may be a necessary precursor to romance,
then I notice her ear — lovely, small,
the great neatness of it, the sort of ear
I am very much already in love with,
and how everything she says now sounds better,
smarter because I am admiring that ear,
that is rather like mine — an aural meme of sorts, so,
dizzied by romance's gorgeous besotted-ness: I hear
Austen suggest I'm a narcissist swimming in my gene pool.

My Vegetable Love Shall Grow

for Bart Brassica

Kohlrabi

Beseeching the sun, kohlrabi grows
a dozen arms, lank and limber supplicants.
Is it scared of being buried, that shape
is fate? Beseeching, kohlrabi grows
a tuberous torso, then lank and limber,
calling all its brassy allies to arms?

Cauliflower

I knew we'd been estranged when my
five year-old called you white broccoli
but it was kiss and make up melon-cauli-
flower, bathing you in cheesy béchamel,
or roasting your white cranium into nut brown
sweetness, blanching your nubbled florets,
steaming your white head into a transcendent state,
and me, colly-wobbled, taste buds, again, all ears.

Barns in Charlevoix

I like the barns, their air of constancy,
their un-renovated geometry, their wooden deshabille,
that they have high hipped roofs — and windows

set without regard to symmetry — that they are unpainted,
the wood grey or brown with age, with parts that lean in
or out, that some are abandoned but endure, that one

imagines the light inside — diffuse and murky
or the doors opening wide and a sudden shaft
of afternoon pouring like honey into dark tea

and the scent of hay and sweet apples on a high
shelf — the horse and cow smells fading,
old leather bridles, iron parts of farm machines,

sump oil, the ammonia of mice,
rough hessian sacks of chaff and bags
of chicken feed, that time here re-collects itself —

sleeps like Keat's Autumn on the bales — and
does not wake but dreams of waisted frocks,
wide hips, foals, fiddles, harvest suppers.

In the Key of Milk

Half pints and quarter pints — translucent meniscus,
film around the neck, whiter than white porcelain,
simplicity. Shoulder sun-warm

I'm at le Ferme and breakfast; a distant row of pines
might be a façade of paper trees, but you find inside
the thicket-edge a forest true to rumour. Step in,

the ground is pine-needle dry, aspen leaf crisp
mushroom dark, interlaced with paths, a bench
for a badgers' picnic, chairs for the porridge bearers,

a rabbit hole for Alice. But no woolly wombats
and Gretel will not be scared by a red-back.
Beyond these woods on the Baie-Saint-Paul,

a flock of ducks, a wooden ship wrecked by fire,
a wrack and flotsam-edged cusp of sand,
opaque water, tanker silhouettes in the distance.

No Longer Your Poem

No longer am I your poem, your breath has left me,
I am grafted to this page. Go, from now on I keep
verbs to myself, you can no longer tamper
with my pronouns. Punctuate someone else.
I divorce myself from you, disown you
and your pencil thin prerogatives.
I am ex-postulate, travelling, camping out,
an independent poem.
You remember me as this static page,
your lazy snapshot memory that erases
my early life, my permutations and later travels.
Are we each a single dose to each other?
I am no longer yours, it is my breath
that holds up the spaces on this page.
I keep your word? You do not.
I am now thou to thee.

Farewell to Rotten Boughs

for Thomas Wyatt

Climb no more rotten boughs,
send no more letters Thomas, I've grown
new leaves and fret no more for last summer's
fruit, the dusk may set its calm acres before your gaze
and I will forgo all sighs and breathings, each pin
of the ticking I have un-plucked from where we were stitched
together upon evening's quilt, night no longer drowns me,
the lake, as cold as Lazarus, bleeds the blueness
from my lips, write to me no more Thomas,
I am the trout, the gilly weed and cannot read,
write to me no more.

Bundanon Haiku

A fly bows two viola
chords in each of my ears.
A concerto follows.

Ink on my sleeve
oh the exasperation
of clothes.

I have known
toasters, like
burning caskets.

I burp lemon essence
from eating cake
that is lemonless.

Lost in haiku
time, I run
to poem class.

Tokyo Set

What Do Fish Think of Rain

Rain is falling water,
the sky trying to become
the river.

Umbrella Day: The Spoke'n World

Clear plastic, odd florals, patterns, solid
colours, checks, one royal red satin, bring
their cargo of jeans, suits and gumboots, running
with rain, topped with bamboo, metal
or wood, a world of edged parabolas,
one clear with pink spots,
black for salary men.
I see the same umbrella twice —
good luck.

Myogadani Subway Station, Maramouchi Line

The embankment, concrete diamonds edged with moss, slopes down
to the platform. Theo's eyes, flick, flick, watching sleep coming
he falls asleep, elbows resting on knees, chin resting on one palm,
umbrella held loose in the other.

Kyoto Set

The Six Objects that Girls in Kyoto Must Possess
Cell phone, bicycle,

boyfriend, playtime,

two pairs of high heels.

Ikumatsu Ryokan
Folding away the futon the tatami mat is still

warm from my sleeping self. We've slept in a row,

like silk worms waiting for wings, in a cocoon

of quilt and futon lined with white cotton.

Wheat Gluten Sticks with Red Miso and Fox tail Millet
Fox tail millet, one sees the petite teeth of the vixen,

biting tiny bones of wheat,

her tail upright in the autumn morning.

How the Universe Begins
Look into a clear suimono, objects floating

in a transparent sea: eat the shrimp mousse,

rings of carrot, a bundle of green leaves,

an umbrella stick of mushroom. Leaving only

the invisible containing a world of flavor,

the transparent alphabet of soup.

Coffee Shop Selling Vintage Railway Paraphernalia
Kyoto, on Shinmozen Dori, with my husband drinking coffee
from Noritake cups matched to the beans,
a donut packet's counsel – *Enjoy the rich taste which
has been loved* – grows slowly more profound.

Sakamoto Noodle Shop
We stop for a bowl of noodles, the broth arrives, slightly
 peppery, after talking in circles tangled like ramen.

Hot Springs Bath
The women bathe chattering, with only
a pink towel resting on the head,
each with nothing to show the world but skin.

In the Lake Viewing Room
Fires lit on the jetty, flames guttering into separate rushes,
each fire tongue gone in an instant while the brazier burns
on water and in air until all fuel is spent.

A rim of lights punctuates the lake's edge, close by
their colours trail into the water, miles away
their reflections are invisible.
Lake Biwa

Rider

She is playing polo
in the Tang Dynasty
— fist tight, head
 turned, hair swept up
in an elegant comma,
suddenly she shouts
Yiah Yiah, who has turned
my horse to clay?

Art Gallery of NSW

Spring Raining

Suspended in a hammock
reading crime, the sky's a clear
and perfect blue, the cut grass grows
green beneath me. Splashed by
a mysterious rain, I see a noisy miner —
Manorina — flying past has frisked off droplets
from her bath recently re-filled by me.
Vicariously dampened, I read on.

Manorina melanocephala, the Noisy Miner.

The Horse's Leg

Mrs Gaskin Stifle-Hock rode her mare
at the trot, she asked in places misanthropic
would they feed her horse on wine?
Did they decline?
They offered hock in a casket; the horse
went home in a basket. Mrs Gaskin
was in two minds; should she leg it home alone,
or wait until her pony phoned.

Lady Penelope Goes to the Speech Therapist

Still a bit wooden, says Mrs T,

try this vowel exercise

un   er irs aa O

un   er irs aa O

Lady P stares a second too long

at Mrs T's lips,

which are not moving at all.

Lady P turns her head, runs

her little feet this way and that,

narrows her eyes, she wants to cry

this is dubbed isn't it? isn't it ?

then a voice off-stage calls CUT.

Colour in Black and White Westerns

Randolph Scott was colour blind
but had a fine sense for grey graduations,
a fine sense of tonality, and now
no-one would know he wore
a cerise double weave shirt, a purple
leather holster and pants with so much canary
in the yellow the back-lot birds trilled
to see him. Extras got a special
rate to deal with the nausea
his colour tension inflicted on closed sets,
and, to boot, there were given a good slug
of rye, to steady their eyes.
Sometimes the props fell apart from his glare,
but take away technicolour,
and that pea green hat is pure hero.

Quaver

If some distances, say those between x and y
(where x and y are points on a sphere),

are constantly recalibrated as x and y's positions
on the circumferential lines that connect them

oscillate, for example if x is in London and moves
to Paris and y (oh dear y) is in Borneo

and goes on to Omeo, as this set of distances approaches
the infinite, and as x wavers and might think of y, and y (oh, y)

sometimes thinks of x, what part of this quavering,
quasi-infinite set might be attributed to x and what to y?

A History of Zero

Obol

Obol the coin which beggars
cursed in their cups, that children
might turn over in optimism,
in case it was not Obol. So little
value, a purse heavy with you,
a metaphor for disappointment.
Two obols, shorthand
for a worthless marriage.
A coin with so little metal
you floated on ponds, where
even a fish scale sinks.
Some said you might blow away
like dust in the breeze, others
quipped, no such luck. Neat,
round, concise, you were a tab
for merchants leaving your round
0 on the sand table, suggesting
that place has value, your indent
a nudge to invent something
very like you, to prove
that less is more.

A Hint

Hanging in its waxy ways,
scintilla to scimitar,
scimitar to circular,
then the waning,
edging back the other way
till it's the new zero,
a blank, sunless space
maybe edged with earthshine
a monthly metaphor
the moon, its obverse face being
what you can't see, can't touch
that pulls up the oceans,
menses, seeds. a recidivist blank
space in the lunar calendar,
keeping its place when absent, a hint.

The Zero Waits

I sidled so close to the numbers
that a molecule couldn't get between
us but still they were haughty, too rigid
and superstitious to acknowledge me.
I took to loitering in sentences —
once the Irish had made some space
between the words — hoping some Latin scholar

would get the idea, and decipher me,
notice how like the alpha the numeric is.
I planned what they would say
when they figured out how I could
stop their ledgers from imploding:
Oh, (I fantasized) *this thing, this nothing*
is a mighty scaffold, the Atlas of maths,
an architect almost blasphemous
in its implications — the compositor of calculus.
Then they might have realised I had been waiting
in sly spaces, by abacus beads as they slide,
in empty rooms and know that nothing,
nothing beats the patience of zero.

Moors Come Bearing Zeros

Wrapped inside rolled carpets, puffed by careful caliphs,
quietly biding time on the hands of be-ringed beauties,
infill for arches, all those lovely ovals of placement, orchestrated
to underline zero's beauty, all these things the Moors bring.
The mean of all positive and negative integers, the neutral,
unassuming yet powerful, *cfir* — zero, steps into Spain, the dark
prince of numbers, and quietly surveys what the local
numbers need: nothing, and with humble grace delivers.

Things I Do in My Spare Time

I linger in smoke rings, hold apart musical
notes, empty the thin shells of vowels,
tangle ganglions into knots and plaques
of nothingness, erase memory, void
neural space. It's me that blanks stares, clears
the meditating mind, Buddhists hold me dear,
and I them. Mostly I watch the neighbours,
the palpable, the abstract, the virtual. I study
their particular solidarities. One will always be
measuring itself against another, calibrating,
estimating, counting one thing for another, while I
remain just me, immeasurable, infinitely empty.

Venice 1299

The Doges' ban on the use of zero, the place marker,
that genius for sleight of nothing, is rolled back,
the last bastion of primitive caution
is flattened by that big Zero,
0 it comes out fighting, nothing is too much for it,
nothing can stop it and the Western economy
starts its slide into the virtual.

Good for Nothing

nothing shared is nothing gained
nothing tastes the same as nothing-made
think nothing of it, think nothing
divide by nothing, then multiply by nothing
nothing to do and nothing to say
too many nothings spoil the nothing
a nothing in time, saves nothing
spare the nothing and spoil the nothing
nothing from nothing leaves nothing
two nothings make a nothing
like grains of nothing through the nothing-glass
a fool and his nothing are soon nothinged
many nothings make nothing work
red nothing, yellow nothing
the quick brown nothing
jumped over the lazy-o

Portal

Keats glances off, shy of understanding
the second part of negative capability.
To thrum on any wall, testing for hollowness, to find
a space you can transpose everything into
you need to conceive of the perfect aperture. You need me,
the paradoxical portal, the door that does and does

not exist. I am the little lens that magnifies the more
you know me, the rabbit hole in the poet's pocket.

India's Patent Application

Mr Ravi Kunnar Kenneti, representing India has filed
a claim to patent zero with the European Patent Office
noting that Western nations' unlicensed use — a profligate
squandering — of zero must stop. He states that
all zeros are the intellectual property of their inventor
Mohammed ibn-Musa al-Khowarizmi and his heirs
who being citizens of India and of such a multitude that
their rights are both the true concern of the Indian Government
and the patrimony of the Indian people. As such the al-Khowarizmis
assert their patent right to zero. All persons and any freelance equation
that wants to use a zero or zeroes will need to apply and buy disposable
or single-use zeroes from the al-Khowarzmis. Injunctions will be sought
to stop householders, financial users, schools and institutes
from saving left over zeros from one financial season to the next.

*The European Patent Office (EPO) is about to grant 30 patents on plants derived from
conventional breeding to Monsanto and its affiliated companies. Many of the patents
claim vegetables such as tomatoes, peppers, cauliflower, carrots and lettuce.*

In a Jaipur Guest House

The traffic noise flows in — drone of an out-of-tune sitar,
a bellow made from a smashed oboe, a cello whose sound board
was warped by a curse, and a basket of broken bells begging for alms
cross with a flugelhorn trampled by a truck
as a clarinet with its stops stuck by dung, reed broken,
complains and complains that the squeeze-honk of a bugle
played by man with black lung is biting its ear, each sharpening
note a discord of nails running down a tarred blackboard
with hand brakes squealing, begging for any mercy, any coin,
a safe crossing, an untouched overtaking, a breath of clean air.

The Game

The pigeon keeper is courting you with candy seed,
with cooo-tooo-kooo-coo, consonants virtually nothing
but ties to hang those o's on. You look lost,

gullible, perched on the terrace wall while the flock
that flew in with you settle, peck, startle and revolve,
birds walking blithely in and out of cages.

You, white bird, mottled with iridescent flecks
of malachite, black barred wings, fine black beak,
arcing keel: you pace, approach. More seed, more

k-oooo, more time and when you step up
to the water bowl, I think you're done for Visitor,
you have eaten the treats and now you drink, hesitate —

maybe a bath? The pigeon keeper flashes out a net,
its bamboo loop like a snow shoe and that is that.
Ignominy for you, shame for your owner: a ransom
to your trapper and candy seed for his raiding party.

Old Delhi, India

Two Bridges near Hoi Ann

Two bamboo bridges, both owned by three families,
criss-crossed poles, river deep, joined by mere bamboo
which moans as you cross it,

a xylophone without a tune, calling
on the river, every other note, to let you go,
and every second note to take you.

Wing Chair in Hanoi

Wing chair in black leather
why do you slowly slink
your sitter to the floor?

Suggestion Box for the Australian Kiteflyers Society

A broom kite and a mop kite to clean the skies

An umbrella kite in case of wet weather

Victoria Sponge kite, of course so light it flies

Dust mote kite, tiny but persistent, lofts on a sneeze

Homing kite, set to pigeon

Bread kite, browns nicely at heights

Icarus kite that waxes lyrical

Surfboard kite that will idle for a thermal

Straw kite that when huffed and puffed at

reverses to reassemble as a house

Sheep dog kite that rounds up stragglers

The Franklinator that shocks key players

Bowler Hat kite that's self-doffing

Gossip kite that flies on innuendo

Venetian kite that sings O Sole Mio

Glass kite that throws stones

Sunnies kite that shades its flyer's eyes.

Ice kite that brings spring showers

Stroke Correction

For Charmian Frend

Rough weather, I'm in Balmoral's dim khaki bay with its waves
a choppy matrix in two minds as to come and go.

I've swum the long-ways length of beach with ham fists and crossed
ankles, borne up by buoyancy and saliently salted, tugged at by currents.

The bay bears buoys with yellow heads that have the noddies, slime
and barnacles below their plimsoll. I take a bead on one and two masts

that frame it, as the swells take turns to block the view then
give it back, I'm swimming out, hands going for the catch, relaxed

there and back, where my feet can touch the sand. I wonder am I tired?
and remember my first class composition, lauded for the sentence,

'I lay in the shade, tired and happy after my long swim.' I imagined
the pleasant weight of accomplishment, the spot at Ettalong

where I saw myself, careless then that I could not swim, but now
the words right themselves, retrospectively correct. Swim on.

Watery Havens in the House

Shower

Stall of steam, esteemed stall

of steam, wonderful of clean

surcease of sweat, surfeit

of revery, musical box

of ablution, acoustic cube,

lux mist-ifier.

Bath

Watery sarcophagus,

tiny temperate sea

little lake of suds-topped

languor, chaise-lounge

of H two O, Archimedes'

think tank, serene predecessor

of turbo-spa, little mother

of the dirty.

Garden Hose

Snake in the grass,

prompter of summer

water fights, saviour

of plants, drip-o-

later.

Sprinkler

Errant, banished water
twirler, soaker of lawn
and odd-times laundry,
plying 3-D spiral graphics,
gravity your aid-de-
camp, summer's pluvious
60's playmate.

Learning another Language

Folding laundry, parsing tea-towels
and conjugating my husband's socks,
a frill, a fritillary, a flotilla of Spanish hovers
like it could be mine, like listening to
my of-age daughter, saying something
whose meaning that, at first, I do not
understand. An eager learner, the scaled-down
hearing skills I put to use interpolating,
guessing a line of best fit, I am a crucigramist
of syntax, a dab hand at that time delay
loop where it takes a minute, to appraise,
rerun *las palabras*, to dis-assemble.
Oh. I see now that one's own
is the most confounding language.

Pre-Crastination

the house is full of starting points
corn on the floor, granola seeking berries
you could do more, there's a book upstairs
but then the plants implore, water! me! more!

berries stain granola milk, corn on the floor
inspector noun? that book upstairs implores
detection is the crown of fiction, ignore the corn
floor seeks new broom, nouns need nude room

the house is full of floors, berries seeking same
I could do more than read the book of stairs
a bowl of water wears a supple skin of sun
outdoors, the hose lies, a treble clef on grass

a supple sum implodes, time is a new broom
that sweeps away the present, indoors
is full of lives in drawers, books on floors
the noun inspector goes outside to check,
a trebled length of grass now hides the hose.

Four Capital City Forecasts

Moistly sunny, thatchy patches in the early west
tending towards chance in the north, partly
showered with early mornings. Light clearing

in the evening. Isolated afternoons, partly partly,
clouds becoming eggy, a dance of fog tending
northwest. mostly days, some nights at fifteen isobars.

Summary warnings, fresh at times, chance
of southern suburbs, slow moving Thursdays
with frost around 100 knots. Light words easing.

Diary of a Comma

today, dizzy, first here,
then there, taken out,
put back, deleted
still better to see
the world than always
to stay at Qwerty Place
longing for some ink,
pixels, a page, only
not, please, please,
not another poet.

Asides on a Semi Colon

Half puffed, side-ways winker,
beloved of the discursive thinker,

still tether-able and tolerably useable
when pushed over; colon's half-sister,

comma's half-stutter the ahem in the sentence,
hallmark of lawyers, regulators, the list-prone;

hiatus that does not wait, but says,
no, please, line up, there's space.

Complaints of a Question Mark

Oh my back is killing me, condemned to be
the Quasimodo of the sentence, accused
of being querulous then rhetorically eschewed.

English sentences me to be an apercu
and so, coming in too late, I cop the blame
for lazy readers' lack of interrogative tone.

My role? Half-crone, half-know it not,
big headed you might think but but but —
I'm not a quisling undermining words,
a judge's aide-de-camp, a phrase's little

anglopoise lamp, I see myself as vivacious
enquirer, lucidity adjutant and no mere cat's tail
or hang-dog of the uncertain. What other
punctuator can, solo, make sentence?

Ellipsis Non Loquitur

for Noela

Triplets with a stutter, withholding pause, you're
a no-don't-say non sequitur, suggestive
of room for more, awkward hiatus,

cliff hanger for a clan-destination,
sand in the sentence's tennis shoe,
remorse-less code, mum's these spots,

say-me-not's, flat parabola of inference,
join the dots, coy non-carper, O-mission
that sets out to say something between zero

and infinity, nascent word and number buds,
pi-taler, under-dotter, cling-wrap of the unsaid,
equivocating threesome, blanc de blanc

de blanc, someone's dotage, unassailable unsayer,
MIA, guesser what-er, lisping gap that nearly hisses,
 triodox, tell you later, coy failure to …

Abusing the Full Stop

You're too bossy with your I-say-stop
and Oh-that's-enough, the sentence's
overseer, a trip point that seeks

to end it all, punctilious micron of ink,
more than a comma doing overtime,
grammatical cattle-dog, should be

disambiguator, I don't want your that's
that, your chummy closeness with the last
word, your implicit partnership

with the Upper Case, your brinkmanship
with the line break, your instruction to break
here, little stab of stop, party pooper,

your inverse frequency a barometer of syntactic
complexity, peas in the paragraph's matrices —
even, even when as a last resort

I, brainwashed automaton, might,
typing on my Olivetti, sprinkle
you about like putative confetti,

or jab or dot or punctuate the page
with quink — one might think I like you —
no — I'm casting round for an hiatus,

give me em dashes, sighs and semi-colons
why should I be cut short by a spot?
a low-line inter-punct, prequel to decimal places,

post-fall disowned diacrit, com's high tech
partner, alloy-er of abbreviation, period drama:
in a poem one's company two's a crowd..

The Teasdale Cup

My motives? Free periods to prepare,
spent in empty classrooms, making
the most of unsupervision, ardently

not-preparing, concocting jokes,
jumping out of windows. Then
the morning teas, tables of cream

buns, chocolate milk, dreadful scones
so dosed with bicarb they fairly
sizzled on the tongue.

Was it the other speakers, the soon
to be Suzie Quatro tragic, later stalker,
then loner, acne, thick lenses, bobbing

larynx, who declared he would sand-blast
the Wyong Team, but was struck mute,
a hideous apoplexy writhing in his throat

while first and second speaker's side-line
prompts defined futility. The lovely Irish
Monica who, in a whirlwind of rebuttal, ripped

all her notes to fine confetti that she flung,
emphatic, on the boards, disposing thus
of both their argument and any hope of summary.

The away-trips in Mr Rouse the English teacher's ancient
v-dub, where he gives us oranges, and Denis pulls
the ashtray out of its socket trying to stuff in the peel?

Mr Rouse, both agitated and amenable
says *just throw it on the floor*. Debatable
even now what set me off in that quest to win

The Teasdale Cup. If I had to say it was whim
or disposition, my answer would depend
if I am in government or opposition.

Black and White in Swans

Though in theory and in practice
I know swans come in black
and white, watching the white ones'
long necks upside downed into
Winchester water meadow's lake
or the whole bird upright
on the Avon, it seems surprisingly
wrong; some inner mechanism
in me whispers: all swans are black.

Sherwood Green

A woman standing barefoot in her underwear,
two weeks now since I took in
her casual gesture, the exact economy
of her hands shaking into shape a dress
of Sherwood green, that flares then flattens
on command, reversed onto the ironing
board, as seamlessly the seams fall into place,
one hand finessing with a casual caress corrects

the lay, the other glides the iron across, once,
twice. The dress almost dances up
and before it slips over her arms and hips,
it turns a single pirouette, while she checks
for creases that now do not exist. Hard to say
what has more grace, the ironer or the dress.

Les Lolitas

They are the Les Lolitas, two seasons
new, pale blue, kid-like leather,
a pair that fit my feet like dancing pumps,

they're dirty now being so down
to the ground, the toes scuffed at the point.
Baby brogues, sometimes when I tie your laces

I wait a moment, tracing how my hands
act as automatons, an effect so licentiously
pleasant, that I've seen myself undo each,
so I can retie the bow, redo the double knot.

Parka

The anglicans, always a finger in every sin,
have set up the lie that to do something
that feels quite delicious is suspect —
a sin, for which you'll pay later —
hell or no hell. So at home, when I put on
my down-parka wearing naught else but
undies, the morning wonderfully
autumnal (a word I've been waiting years
to get into a poem), it feels too good to be legal,
so warm and so soft, that I spend some minutes
parading and patting, warm and regal,
zipping it up before ruefully taking it off.

The Pattern

Bus drone drawn, knitting
in a slough of travel, garter
garter, baby cardi, sleeve
and back. The rhythm of stocking.
on and on, and those intermittent
movements where the little finger
lifts a loop —off skein— of thread
that lies as light, lies as silk,
says progress, says prospect,
and all the time the pattern waits;
a finite length of yarn ahead.

January, off Broke Road, the Winery

The casuarinas gossip softly, swapping notes,
over a ponderous puddle of brown tea.
Late afternoon, stare hard at the mountains

and they reprint on the clouds. Frogs orchestrate the night
singing like drunken soldiers, for love and their lost tails.
That fat fool — there, over the vines — the full moon, ignore him.

Last night's Christmas beetle's stranded, stilled, past rocking.
Righted, it locks one claw into my notebook.
Ferguson, the tractor, is elephant-coloured, the king of the grass,

stubborn to start, a simple servant who barks hard, chokes in diesel,
then gets on with it. The creek swims with a tannin gouache, and children
tinted orange, who slide under its slow folds, splash back up in seal skins.

January grapes hum into ripeness, the sun-blistered
golden ones, culled, feed the vines. The cockies with a taste
for chardonnay send out emissaries to talk turkey with the gas gun.

The vines are swagged and clustered, hung and decorated,
draped and dripping with grapes, that clarify, forgetting
chlorophyll for gold and red, stalks hardening to sticks,
the skins blooming with the idea of wine.

June, off Broke Road, the Winery

I

Broke Road, bar coded by sapling sapling sapling,
a running argument, that with each returning curve
seems more familiar, while winery shingles, hinging

on the verge, shout choose me, me, me.
Then the sound of gravel complaining of the tyres
and vice versa. We arrive.

A few new green shoots, mistaking temperature
for time of year, waving, gaily waiting
for the secateurs. The trees are all on nodding terms

with each other and ourselves. The Olive Lunch crowd
mix the peplum-esque with boots, boots and boots.
Strato-cumulus roll in from the East.

Athena, Goddess of Olive Oil, sees them off. A long table
marches on near five hundred legs, staying
where it is, in the groove of clinking glasses, effervescent

banter and chitterage; a hiatus where hats are found
for the hatless. The afternoon warms us in its lap.
Cool green puddles are wiped away with bread and fish.

One long Elysian moment, then there is nothing but empty chairs,
napkins, lip-synced empty glasses, the light a liquid amber contracting
to the west. We pivot between being and remembering.

Walking back to digs, a circle of legs that dance
a hop, and twitch and lurch, hurl a pagan chant at the sunset.

II
Light of morning, two galahs fly out of a mistletoe-
tasselled gum, then a pair of eastern rosellas leave on two
whims. From Ferguson's pond frogs claxon-ate.

June picks up my page, shakes out a memo to the winter wind: *you're late*.
Late too, the roses hoodwinked by warm May days now drop their petals
revealing naked hips. The sky's a perfect cerulean hemisphere tucked

in behind a ragged rug of hills. A man's shadow rakes the dew.
A magpie kardeloos — *what'll we dooo*. Rows of vines converge
to show just how perception gives Euclid's geometry a raspberry.

The horizon jammed with all those things — mountains, half-moons,
                                        clouds —
that distance leaves there. Four ducks make their way off stage, a dog
barking in the distance, never shows.

Three burros are staring through a fence, behind them a stand of

                                                         casuarinas,

felled, have stopped talking altogether. The vintage cools in

                                                  stainless steel,

two years' worth waiting in tanks and barrels.

The first car of the morning touches down for sips of semillon, shiraz
and port, the men's elbows polishing the Oregon, the women soberly
considering the view.

October, Off Broke Road, The Winery

Burning the Canes

There's a Lama paddock out the kitchen window
and, as the afternoon wears on, shadows
stretched by Sydney Long.

The birds start up, spotted pardalotes, wrens,
top-knot pigeons, trilling, whistling — ayk ayk
burble, chortle — the blue wren's tail a frisky

fan that works three times as hard as him—
the Right Busy Grass Inspector.
A white egret punctuates the reeds

near Adam's Road, three paddocks off
October vines quilt the slope diagonally.
A makeshift lake has set up in a corner block

where three horses ignore their own reflections
a pee-wee pewits bright & sharp as tin,
the pump kicks in, the roses hit full throttle,

light the end of vine rows, spiral galaxies of petal-novas,
yield drowsy beauties that hang indolent in jars and vases,
the band eases into the fourth bracket of the blues,

a table-full of punters amble off, one waves a hand,
ample hips shifting to the shiraz's syncopation
A boy, hair so white it's faintly green, knees scutched

with dirt, speaks charming not-yet-English, leaves
an oily rouge of pasta sauce on his mum's skirt
Around the back, three kids play in the sprinkler,

each drop a bright cold rainbow. The air hangs time like aspic.
The canes, smoldering in the fretwork barbecue
burn down to white leaves of fairy paper.

10,000,000 Years Ago We Take to Drink

Ethanol, un-metabolisable — hardly wise
for animals eluding carnivores or swinging
on lianas — fermented in the fruit that dangled,
toxic, from low boughs, or fell in gelid sacks
from likely trees, and as forests shrunk, even less
of these, leaving rotters, a niche supply
of punch-drunk fruit. Then that singular
mutation, a jackpot forty-fold activation
of alcohol dehydrogenase, so it leans its elbow
on the bar, *my shout, this one's on me,*
and sip by nip, our improved enzyme rendered
meals from poteens of fallen fruit and now turns
them into party favours, analgesics, the nectar
of the gods, hilarity, not to say next-day-at-sea,
and addiction. Some say wine is evidence
that gods exist and want us to be happy,
but this is proof that inside us all there is
a screw that winds the cork from every bottle.

Comparative Anatomy

Palms down I study the blue lines that wend the blood
into my hands; the left's ulnar artery branching much closer
to the fingers than the right's whose veins are more pronounced.
Though it's years now since it was only the right that wrote,
the right is still more dextrous but then as I type this

I know the left does qwerty quick as a brown fox, lends a hand
for jars, if it is gauche with toothbrush and vacuum cleaner
it's fine with forks, and here, on the page it wants to get a better
share of letters. Maybe it aspires to darker things, the redacted.
It says my blood is the same as yours mr right hand man.

Morning at Middle Harbour, February 2015

A silence is cast over Grotto Point, over its under
skirt of sandstone, silence cocoons the motor boat
speeding over the Point's silver-green shadow,
and silence washes over Edward's Bay, encasing the swimmers,
arm by arm, swaddling the board paddlers one stroke at a time,
even sneaking under the footsteps of runners on the sand
and the volleys of joggers on the Esplanade,
while a silent hubbub fills the café, and my toast arrives,
suggesting a map of Australia, and I look around
my plate for Manus Island but it is completely lost to sight.

Karelia

Every day two villages disappear
(insert blank space here)
Phwaaa. It's summer but here are

snow drifts in attic corners,
great banks resting where the church
(insert blank space here)

has turned into splinters
of silver wood and holey ghosts.
Every day two villagers disappear

[insert two blank spaces here] so
pray against arsonists and careless
cigarettes. The village (blank space)

is declared neperspektivnie — to be
liquidized for lack of proper prospect.
The fields are given to the crows.

Every day two more crows appear
[insert black spaces here and here]
to wander through houses like

the winter wind, that mills history
to a rough grey grit. The village shop stocks

(insert blank space here)

and vodka, and soon these bottles
disappear into empty stomachs
and move on. Two bull-dozers appear.

(Insert blank space
here and here
and here)

Primer

Before you start this poem please read this list of words:
twilight, happiness, wonder, fearless, content, success.
Now take this short survey:

How long is it since you've read a fearless poem at twilight?
Do you feel very happy or just happy reading?
Is your day a success if it contains a moment of literary wonder?
What is more important to you, a poem's content or its form?

The first star hangs out its shingle, jazz piano drifts in
from a room above, the air is still, a fearless blue pervades,
somewhere a man paces a field, speaking quietly to himself,
surely in metaphors, rehearsing each word, a synaesthesia
squeezing thought into sound. Then he walks
southward, dwindling into the distance and the dark.

Variation on Wang Wei's poem

We said the last words
in the inn for the dying elders
before the dense blue of sky

and sea, two curtains, one old
patient blurring the view
Of course I had bought flowers

and you your dignity, a slight
annoyance at being encumbered
by tubes. We spoke of eternity,

in the jewelry sense, and laundry.
I held your middle finger,
lightly stroking a space free of tape.

Now I concentrate on remembering your voice.
Past the skyline, today's rain falls
chattering, dampening the dust.

Artichokes

She asks if they can buy artichokes,
at a roadside stall and, in a rare moment
of convivial mother-teen daughter

agreement, they're bought
and taken home. In search of the heart
they pulled off the hard leaves, evicted

the sharp choke. In the end everything
was discarded. They found nothing
palatable, but it was no great loss,

and bemused, the search for the heart
was turned into what at first was
an anecdote, and later, an augury.

Caricia's Quarter Acre

Come, she says We follow,
past the sour orange tree,
the avocadoes hanging like fattened
exclamation marks, past the overhang
of mangos from the neighbour's,
to a dank under-story and the smell
of ripening despair,

where a pig sleeps, penned, hemmed
on every side by Besser blocks,
one trough, in which Caricia pours
some water, a scoop of meal,
commends to us the tastiness of pork
and the pig clambers to its feet,
looks up beseechingly. Oh pig,
I'm sorry there s only this.

Vinales, Cuba

The RMC Gunn Veterinary Science Building

Tagging along on weekends to check
the automatic stirrers, the slow
chuff of a lab milling experiments,

the assays and isolations, the colonies
of drosophila, and in the room
beyond a strange murmur,

and as they said don't go in there
my hand was on the door
and like Pandora I opened it

and hundreds of lambs looked
at me and instantly the volume
of their bleating made me shut

the door, but they continued,
cued for food and stuck inside cages.
Outside the Sunday afternoon

gamboled on, the oval's verdancy
throbbing light in waves, and a team
in cricket whites going out to field.

Intensive Care

A day contrite, for making such a grim, knifey mess.
The doctor says, he's knicked his heart, the pericardium's
beleaguered. He's been de-warfarinised, stitched up,
bolstered with this tube, that ventilator.

Free helicopter trip, his view only some black swirl
inside his eyes. Or so I guess. No point they say, too risky to try
to stitch the heart, it should mend itself, scar over.
So it does, a day contrite, and then back to it

the doctors being foreigners, the nurses not so good,
and him, going downhill, visitors not quite the right ones —
one has aged, the other's not put on any weight,
the food is shithouse (I second that). We can go

he doesn't want to hold us up. I say we will, when
it suits us, and stay a bit. He brightens up at
baby photos, frets about the weeks ahead
that he had been so desperate to avoid. Leaving

I hold his hand for a moment, its shape
still the same as the man who quizzed me
on social studies, lobsters from Geraldton, coal
from Collie. Looking back he's asleep
before we leave intensive care.

The Man in the Bottle

It is not clear if we ever understand,
one talks, the other nearly answers.
Settling into a polite distance, insulated

by a length of phone line, relieved of each
other's actuality, are these chats or circumlocutions?
He says he's having trouble breathing

and I can hear how his enunciation is bastardised
by lack of breath as if by beer. The subject
never strays too far from the weather, degrees,

humidity, no-one's fool that sun — coy by turns,
the wind's sharp elbows, long sleeves, another
jumper, the acclimatization to a diet of frozen dinners.

One can get use to many things, that time
is hastening away, and this call is limited
by bathroom trips, take it easy I say,
the answer: that's all I can do these days.

The Rip

Balancing the outboard on its propeller
he shakes it once. My guess is there's less
two-stroke in it than is comforting.
We get underway, set out for blue swimmers
in Brisbane Water. Coming up to Booker Bay,
I'm nervy but brave enough to take the steering

through the play of currents in The Rip.
A pod of dolphins, shepherds or wily economists
of energy, tag the bow break, slipstream
in our wake. Later, idling over lines, I ask
if we have enough fuel to get back. Enough
is such an arbitrary measure.

How Things Reverse Like the Tide

The Rip Bridge ties together two sides of Brisbane Water,
spans a Hellespont and the cincture of the bay — The Rip,
 funnelling the intensity built up in the three miles from the Box's

sandbar edge, a tidal current of swift water skirting Ettalong
and Booker Bay. At twelve in winter jeans rolled up, Bon and I walked
out along the sandbar to the Box, laughing at how far out we were

and still only knee-deep. When the sand caved in beneath me,
and I was rushing off, bobbing and amazed, by quick wit
and the virtue of being taller, Bon plucked me out by the collar,

and so I avoided a trip back to Woy Woy and being drowned along the way.
On the south side of the Rip Bridge a cenotaph to Lieutenant Bradley
quotes his diary 1788: *my men could make no headway rowing*

through the Strait. Standing dead centre on the Bridge
there's a clear view of Cockle Bay, the oyster lease, a punt —
maybe with someone in it, but it's not Dicko or my father.

They sold the lease twenty years ago and Dicko's standing with us,
my father nothing more than photographs, memory and ash — of which
I throw a handful — it puffs up into a ghosty cloud, before dissipating

in the wind, liberating him into the air, the tide. To either side
the water has its good mannered shore, calm and nearly sensible —
but below me it is muscle, rush and torrent.

On Taking Away The Bird Bath To Banish Crows

Like grief the crows don't go. You've tried emptying the water
but no, they still come and leave bread and flesh and bones

in the empty space wanting to marinate their carrion,
willing to wait for rain while they interrogate the bowl's weathered

glaze with cocked eye and wiping beak. So, now you've removed
the bowl itself and still they land and strut and pace

the absent spot, their colic cries from branches, echo-locators,
their hunched and folded darkness a foreboding.

The bowl's removal banishes all other birds — their bathings, friskings,
plays and drinks and dousings. Yesterday you even threw a stone

— one of a series — at two crows, only hitting an empty space.
Now the bowl is interred inside the house. Its clear water's

mirrored eye has gone. Now the only way to see your face
reflected in it, framed by sky, clouds and leaves

is to sift through memory's silt or put it back and refill it
and deal with the grievances of crows.

Dunce

That great dunce the new day arrives
awkward in her blue pyjamas
knowing nothing of what will
happen, not even that by evening
her clothes will be smeared with rust,
streaks of blood, that bruised and pale
she will limp off, over the horizon
nearly forgetting the brilliance
of her azure, the long gold
of her afternoon.

Acknowledgements

Grateful acknowledge is made to the editors of the following journals, anthologies, newsletters and programs in which some of these poems were first published: *All These Presences, Antipodes, The Australian, Australian Love Poems, Australian Poetry Journal, Azul, Canberra Times, Best Australian Poetry 2017, Cordite Poetry Review, Island, No Meek Dress, Meanjin, Poetry Mosman, Open Water Swimming Magazine, Recours Au Poeme, Snorkel, Southerly, VLAK 5, Westerly, Whispering Brook Newsletter, Wombats of Bundanon, Writing to the Wire.*

www.ingramcontent.com/pod-product-compliance
Lightning Source LLC
Chambersburg PA
CBHW030851090426
42737CB00009B/1187